RETRIBUTION OR REHABILITATION

HOPE FOR A LIFE BEYOND MAXIMUM SECURITY PRISON

SUE WILLOUGHBY

First published by Ultimate World Publishing 2022
Copyright © 2022 Sue Willoughby

ISBN

Paperback: 978-1-922828-12-5
Ebook: 978-1-922828-13-2

Sue Willoughby has asserted her rights under the Copyright, Designs and Patents Act 1988 to be identified as the author of this work. The information in this book is based on the author's experiences and opinions. The publisher specifically disclaims responsibility for any adverse consequences which may result from use of the information contained herein. Permission to use information has been sought by the author. Any breaches will be rectified in further editions of the book.

All rights reserved. No part of this publication may be reproduced, stored in or introduced into a retrieval system, or transmitted in any form, or by any means (electronic, mechanical, photocopying, recording or otherwise) without the prior written permission of the author. Any person who does any unauthorised act in relation to this publication may be liable to criminal prosecution and civil claims for damages. Enquiries should be made through the publisher.

Cover design: Ultimate World Publishing
Layout and typesetting: Ultimate World Publishing
Editor: James Salmon
Cover photo image license: rawf8-Shutterstock.com

Ultimate World Publishing
Diamond Creek,
Victoria Australia 3089
www.writeabook.com.au

ABOUT THE AUTHOR

The author, Sue Willoughby, has had a varied past. She originally trained as a teacher, mainly teaching children with intellectual disabilities. Sue also had a passion for teaching reading and enjoyed watching children blossom as they acquired more skills and confidence in reading, deriving a great deal of pleasure from seeing this in action. After selling a business she then taught adults to read. It was through this teaching that a new door opened, and she began working with people that needed healing from the inside while teaching in a drug and alcohol rehabilitation centre. When Sue began working with these people whose lives were sunken in addiction, she realised that she had found the missing piece of the puzzle of her life up until now and her career path slid sideways. These invaluable work experiences then led her to Corrective Services NSW where similar people, convicted criminals, had often also had their lives destroyed by addiction. Although addiction is by far the most common reason that people turn to crime, Sue observed factors such as low emotional regulation, low self-worth, poor communication skills and a sense of hopelessness lead individuals onto the continuous cycle of returning to custody. Sue's ability to connect with a large range of people helped her to work alongside the inmates in a maximum security setting. She has been able to guide the individuals that wanted out of this cycle with strategies and support to build their resilience and face challenges of a new way of living. Sue knew that they could help them fulfill dreams that they held for their lives but were often too scared to pursue. She knew that she could shine light into their prison cell and hope into their future.

Sue alongside her husband, Mark, her partner in life and also business, raised four independent, free-thinking children who are all making positive contributions to society in their own varied ways. Sue still continues to work in a maximum-security gaol in the area of inmate rehabilitation.

TESTIMONIALS

◆◇◆

What transpires behind prison walls is rarely reported with balance and compassion. It's even more rare that such a balanced and insightful view of the good work staff are trying to achieve behind bars surfaces in the public domain. Sue Willoughby's book should be essential reading for anyone with an interest in corrections and for any policy makers who want a real picture of what coal face staff are trying to achieve.
Brad Peebles, Governor, Macquarie Correctional Centre NSW

Throughout the course of this illuminating book, Sue is able to use her many years of experience working for Corrective Services NSW to provide readers with a unique look at life behind bars, and the ways in which the system could be improved to reduce recidivism rates. Sue's own valuable insights demonstrate a great deal of empathy and a clear desire to improve outcomes for prisoners and society alike, and she combines these with the first-hand experiences of a recently released prisoner to offer a fascinating examination of the prison system within Australia.
James Salmon, Editor

Sue Willoughby has provided us with a great insight of steps being taken to encourage rehabilitation and starting a new life for inmates. To show them there is life outside prison walls and there are skills they can learn and take with them.

I found her book very interesting and have enjoyed learning about what happens inside a gaol and the steps being taken to work alongside the inmates.

I especially enjoyed the interview and would like to wish him the very best of luck in the future. It sounds like he is doing great and enjoying his new life. I hope he gets his licence and the car he has dreamed about.

Congratulations Sue on a wonderful book that so many will enjoy and learn about something we normally wouldn't have a chance to.

Julie Fisher, Author

CONTENTS

About the Author	iii
Testimonials	v
Introduction	1
Chapter One: Retribution, rehabilitation and the way we look at punishment	5
Chapter Two: Statistics of incarceration and recidivism	17
Chapter Three: Successful prisons in Scandinavia and Australia	25
Chapter Four: Gaols as a therapeutic community	37
Chapter Five: Motivating change in current and former inmates	45
Chapter Six: Different forms of rehabilitation	53
Chapter Seven: The interview	63
Chapter Eight: The end is just the beginning	73
References	77
Note from the Author	79

INTRODUCTION

——————— ◆◇◆ ———————

This book is written as a discussion about the benefits of working towards rehabilitating inmates from a maximum-security gaol setting. It discusses the two streams of thought in prison management. The first of these is to confine a person in gaol convicted of an offence as a punishment for that offence. The second stream of thought is the idea of rehabilitating criminals whilst incarcerated in gaol, so that when they are released from gaol, they are better equipped to lead a more productive, happier life.

I examine incarceration rates around the world and compare them to our own Australian incarceration statistics, and briefly touch on the statistics of Aboriginal people entering custody within NSW. I also examine the models of different prisons throughout the world that have been able to dramatically reduce the rate at which released inmates return to custody, the principles that underlie these models, and how these principles have made their way into NSW and are now being applied in some gaols within this state.

Corrective Services NSW has led the way in seeking out and implementing these changes into new prison design and followed through with the ethos of positive interactions between correctional staff and the inmates that are held in their care. These same principles are being implemented in all gaols throughout NSW, even if these gaols were not founded on the therapeutic community model. The therapeutic community model in the gaol setting acts as a mini society where the inmates have input into the running of their own community. They are involved in the democratic process of running their community, and this autonomy brings with it both an increased sense in their self-worth and the idea that their actions have influence over the environment that they reside in.

Within this therapeutic community in the gaol environment, activities are designed to further increase this self-efficiency with extensive educational opportunities offered to the inmates. These educational activities are frequently linked to the inmates working in the gaol industries with traineeships. Again, this furthers the effect of the relevance of the education because, by putting the theory into practice, the inmates are undergoing workplace learning. The accumulation of these acquired skills helps to better prepare them for their life after release from gaol.

Although I do work in the prison system and am an employee of Corrective Services NSW, I do not profess to be an expert in offender management and inmate rehabilitation. This book is a snapshot of what I see through my eyes as I engage daily with inmates in the maximum-security gaol where I work. They are all my thoughts and ideas about a job that I perform with passion and dedication with the satisfaction that I can enable positive change. I can bring HOPE into inmates' lives and let

INTRODUCTION

them see that their dreams are achievable. I have a wonderful job. I see these individuals as people who have made some mistakes in their lives. And if they can learn a lesson from this mistake, then they may be able to look back and see that it has given them the chance to reflect and grow. And what person can say that they have never made a bad choice in their life that they later regretted? And what is our society if it does not give a person a second chance?

Within this book, I tell a little of my own story which led me to the job that I now do. I let the reader know the circumstances that led to a change in my career from classroom teacher to the work I do now within the welfare area. I feel that my job is about HOPE. I give hope to people who sometimes cannot see hope in their own future. I feel honoured to be able to present an interview with an inmate who has recently been released from custody. He speaks highly about the gaol that gave him opportunities to change his ways and free him from the cycle of crime and begin to lead a new life. This man talks about what life is like "on the inside", and the fact that though many people are given opportunities, unless they take them, then these opportunities can just pass them by and their life will remain the same. He also states how proud he is of himself for being able to stay focused on achieving a normal life of going to work, shopping for groceries and enjoying recreational activities with newly made friends and work colleagues. His words bring hope to the prison system, and shed light on the fact that by trialling new ideas in NSW gaols, there is a brighter future for all of us.

CHAPTER ONE

RETRIBUTION, REHABILITATION AND THE WAY WE LOOK AT PUNISHMENT

─────── ◆◇◆ ───────

This is the beginning of a book that is designed to stimulate thinking about the way our society treats our offenders who break the law. Different ideas are put forward for inquiring minds to think about the way things have been done in the past, and to ponder if those same old ways should continue into Australia's future. If society can accept that new, successful ideas have been implemented around the world, it can open up new possibilities for offender management in Australia.

Before we get started, let's take a look some definitions of retribution and rehabilitation.

RETRIBUTION OR REHABILITATION

The word **retribution** comes from the act of taking revenge. Its meaning is defined as "punishment inflicted on someone as vengeance for a wrong or criminal act".

Retribution comes from the Latin word for giving back what's due, be that reward or punishment. But when we talk about retribution, we usually only talk about punishment. The old punishment code of "an eye for an eye, and a tooth for a tooth" is a common example of retribution. There is a school of thought that the punishment should fit the crime. The more severe the crime, the harsher the punishment for that crime should be.

A different way to look at this idea of punishment is to try to **rehabilitate** the offender. Rehabilitation comes in so many different forms and criminal behaviour is such a complex issue that the rehabilitation of that behaviour must take on many different forms. It needs to respond to many different issues, such as the environment in which the offender lives, the environment that the person grew up in, as well the friends and acquaintances that he keeps. Often crime is associated with low socio-economic communities where poverty may lead a person to commit crime because their basic needs are not being met, like shelter and food.

Rehabilitation can be defined as "the action of restoring someone to health or normal life through training and therapy after imprisonment, addiction, or illness".

Looking at rehabilitation, it is so much more than just a word – it's a whole atmosphere that needs to be addressed. Rehabilitation might involve vocational training and/or education. Many of the people who are in gaol right now have had very limited education, so addressing things such as increasing their literacy and numeracy skills so that they can fill out forms can have a huge impact on their life. Other things that need to be addressed aside from a lack of education include a lack of opportunity, lack of housing and lack of money.

Rehabilitation needs to address criminals' thinking – to change their perception. When we look at all human beings, most people have the same desires in life. They have the desire to be loved, to have a connection with other people, with their family, with their community. They want to have meaningful employment, which then gives them a higher feeling of self-worth. Often people want to be respected and looked up to within their community. When they live, and have grown up in poverty, in a criminal environment, then they will often think that the community in a broader context looks at them as useless, worthless beings.

In these next few chapters, we will critically examine the areas of both retribution and rehabilitation. Questions will be asked, and it is up to the reader to find their own answers to these questions. Let the journey begin.

Punishment

Even looking back at the societies of the original Indigenous people of Australia, systems existed to punish people who had done wrong, whether they had stolen from somebody or assaulted them. So, the system of punishing a person for wrongdoing is something that has been in place for thousands of years.

When Australia was colonised, it was set up as a place to send convicted criminals on the other side of the world, also known as a penal colony. Australia is an island, so it was a perfect place to send a person convicted of a crime. Australia has therefore been used for punishment since the first fleet came to our shores in 1788.

From Australia initially being a whole country gaol, other smaller gaols were subsequently set up from within the original country of Australia. Tasmania, originally named Van Diemen's Land, Norfolk Island, and Cockatoo Island in Sydney Harbour were ultimately set up as gaols within the larger gaol of Australia.

Clearly, the idea of punishing people for crimes has been around for a very, very long time. I suppose the question to ask is, if we have been doing it for thousands of years, do we feel that we could do things better? Has it been successful? And if it hasn't been successful, then why do we continue to do the same thing over and over again?

If a person commits a crime, then that person needs to be punished for committing that crime. Often that punishment is being incarcerated, but not always. Sometimes for smaller crimes, or if the person has not had a lot of contact with the law, that person will be given a community order or some other form of detention. For the purpose of this book, however, I am focusing on people who have been committed of a crime and then are sentenced to imprisonment. Imprisonment is retribution for the crime that they have committed.

I went and visited Cockatoo Island recently. It is a very interesting place to wander around. There were cells made of Sydney's iconic and beautiful sandstone. The whole place is majestic, looking over to the Sydney Harbour Bridge and around to Balmain. The water laps at the island's shores. It glistens like a jewel in the crown of our beautiful harbour. As my husband and I wandered around enjoying the view, my heart sank as I looked at the conditions and cells that the offenders had to endure there. One cell was underground. My husband is a little over six-foot tall and he could not stand up in that cell. I tried to imagine a man being imprisoned underground in a cell where he could not even stand up, and with no light – there was not a window, only a small peep hole through the door. It was very dark in that cell.

If you imprison someone in a cell like that, what are you hoping to achieve? Is it just to punish them for the crime they have committed? They may have committed a crime, but that is the front end, entering gaol for a crime. What is the back end? What is society thinking? Yes, if this person has committed a crime then he needs to be punished – the public needs retribution for that crime. The punishment is to be locked away for a certain period of time. But can any of us imagine what it would be like to be in a cell like that for even one month? Imagine if it was for six months, or two and a half years?

So, if we look at the crime as the front end, what is the back end? What are we trying to achieve by locking that person in a cell, locking that person away from society? Is the back end of this question "What will this person be like when they leave that cell or exit gaol?" Will they be the same person that entered that cell? We have isolated that person away from society. We have isolated them from their family. But what are we trying to achieve? Are we trying to say, "You did wrong"? "You need to be punished." Or can we do things a little bit differently? That's probably the point where there is movement from punishment of a crime to rehabilitation of that person, with the end goal to discourage them from committing that same crime again.

Rehabilitation is a very involved process. It is a process that involves many factors related to why that person has committed that crime in the first place. Sometimes the crime is committed out of desperation or pure poverty. Or it may be the other end of the scale, where a person might not be impoverished. They might be greedy. They might have enough food to eat, a car to drive. They might have a house to live in. They may just want more. They may be greedy and not want to work for money but still obtain the things of a higher lifestyle. So, they commit crime to get them. They don't want to wait.

Let's use a car as an example. They may have a car. They can move from A to B. It's not a great car – it may only have a cost a couple of thousand dollars. But they want a bigger, better, faster car. They want one that is worth a lot more money, a car which is a lot more prestigious. They don't want to wait. They don't want to work. They don't want to wait two or three years to put money away and save up, working hard at a job. Are they lazy? They may want instant gratification; they want it now and don't want to wait. Don't want to wait two years to get that car, they want it right now.

Recently, I have been reading John Marsden's book "The Art of Growing Up" about parenting, and I found the whole book, especially the first chapter, very interesting. In the book John writes that the perpetrator of a crime was often, for many years, the victim of that same crime.

In his book, John writes, *"In our society, many of us purport to have all the sympathy in the world for abused children. We weep at their loss of innocence. We understand how it is that many (in some cases all) of the foundations of their lives were ripped from under them by a destructive human bulldozer. We support them with counselling and care. We are horrified as we read stories in the media of children abused by trusted adults.*

That's how it's supposed to work anyway.

Almost in the same breath we denounce child abusers. We call them 'scum', 'filth', 'animals', 'monsters'. We want them to be castrated, locked up for life, executed. 'If I could get my hands on those mongrels,' we say fiercely.... One of the ways we justify this rage is to tell ourselves and each other that we are showing our solidarity and sympathy with the abused children, protecting our own children, even though they are presumably not threatened by people who have already been arrested. 'Think of the children!' as Helen Lovejoy cries at regular intervals in The Simpsons, flapping her arms in helpless anguish. 'Won't somebody please think of the children?'

However, wherever there is great rage, something interesting is always happening. I'm attracted to the thick black smoke of communal rage, because I know that if I can get to the truth within, I'll understand a little more about humanity.

One of the truths about the complex issue of child abuse is that the child for whom we show such support, and the abuser for whom we show such contempt, are the same person. We claim to feel love for the abused child, but when some abused children grow up and start acting out the consequences of their abuse, we react to them with fury and hatred. The abused child who had the foundations of his life so devastatingly damaged will, without support and understanding, grow up continuing to feel frightened and lost. To allay these feelings he may try to recreate a situation in which he felt 'held', and this may include encounters where he was literally held, whilst being beaten, or being seduced into sexual encounter."

So all of a sudden, the coin flips over. That child who has been viewed by society for many years as a vulnerable victim is no longer the victim, but has become the perpetrator of that crime. Now society hates that child, and that child is viewed as a terrible person. He needs to be punished for that crime. Society wants retribution for that crime that has now been committed. Not long ago, however, that same person was a child and was a victim.

That vulnerable child has hit an important period in their life. It's like a disturbance in the flow of water, it's a whirlpool of confusion. They are sucked into this whirlpool, they cannot comprehend what is happening to them. They are spinning around and bobbing up and down, trying to keep their head above water. Their life is full of emotions they have never experienced before. They are in puberty. The lilo flips over and now that vulnerable victim becomes the perpetrator of the crime.

If we examine this more closely, we may see this similar behavior repeated over and over again. A person may have been brought up with abuse, neglect, an environment that does not teach them right from wrong. This may be the prelude to their criminal lifestyle. What is done to them may lead a person into crime because they will "do unto others that which has been done unto them". How is society going to view that child? How are they going to look at that child, who was once a victim and now is a perpetrator of a crime? That same person who has broken the law, and who is now a criminal.

Society can help that person visualise a different life, different to the one they were brought up in. Do they want their own children becoming victims of the similar circumstances that they were raised in? Most parents want a better life for their children then that they've had themselves. Many parents work hard whether they have a lot of money or not much money. They work hard to provide for their children. To give their children a better upbringing than the one that they endured as a child. They love their children. They want to see their children happy and successful.

At this time, a person who has led a criminal lifestyle might start to question their lifestyle and think about what it is that they want for the rest of their life. These questions may start them thinking, "If I don't want to do this for the rest of my life, how can I get out of it when it's all I've known since I was a child? If I want something different, how am I going to go about it, to achieve that different life? I have got no idea because this criminal lifestyle is all I know."

That person is just following the same path that their parents did. So as society, is it up to us to say to them, "You can be a better member of our community. You can help other people. You can become a productive member. You can make legal money and your children can enter into a world that is different to the world that you grew up in. The family that you grew up in does not have to be the same family that your children grew will up in."

It is hard to forgive a criminal for their crime. When we are sad and torn with anguish it seems to come to front of mind to punish them.

The reality is, however, that being a lifelong criminal often just leads to a life of despair. The families of these people become broken and this causes broken communities, and the criminal themself becomes a broken element too.

In recent times, there has been a lot of gang warfare in the streets of Sydney with rival parties shooting from cars in suburban streets. They have sprayed bullets into suburban houses where innocent neighbours reside. There are rival gangs, and sometimes rival families at war with each other, and their gangland warfare produces unsafe communities. This criminal behaviour is producing broken families. Two rival families feuding with each other. It seems that these families are attending a lot of funerals. A brother or cousin is killed first so then that family retaliates. A killing in retribution for a family member assassinated, shot dead in cold blood. Then the first family might attack back, then there is another funeral. Another sad, distorted family grieving for their loss. Both these families lose cherished family members – cousins, brothers, fathers. These are sad and broken families at war with each other. They put innocent suburban residents in danger. Children playing in the street could become victims in these crimes of retribution.

Does this retribution achieve anything aside from tearing families apart by grief and crime? What brings a stop to these killings? We know that it is hard to turn the other cheek. To accept that, even though wrong has been done, more violence and destructive behavior will not lead to a successful outcome, just a continuation of the hurt that has been endured for many years.

As concerned Australian citizens we all have a voice. It becomes every individual's choice whether to have their voice heard. We are lucky to live in a democratic society that values people's responses to situations that they feel could be improved. We have seen Australians play an active part when they felt strongly about whales being killed in our waters. We saw an immediate reaction from the government when shipping of live cattle was stopped in the north of Australia in June 2011 because Australians were appalled at the conditions that these cattle were living in and also slaughtered in. As Australians, we are allowed to voice our opinions. We have to think about and question many different things, and the treatment of our offenders is at the forefront of the discussions in this book.

CHAPTER TWO

STATISTICS OF INCARCERATION AND RECIDIVISM

◆◇◆

In this chapter I am going to examine the statistics of incarceration rates around the world and Australia. I'll begin with an exploration of a term that is frequently used when examining prisons, and that is recidivism.

The official definition of recidivism is: lapsing into previous patterns of criminal behaviour (Maltz, 1984).

When spoken about within the prison system, recidivism is often referred to as returning to gaol. Once an inmate is released from the gaol, recidivism will be the used terminology regarding when, and if, he returns into custody.

Recidivism is something that all societies throughout the world are aiming to reduce. If recidivism rates decrease it is an indicator that the country is doing something positive for this trend to be lower. This may mean that while in custody an inmate has been able to engage with services that have helped him. For example, he may have been able to focus his time in gaol increasing his work skills, so that upon his release he is able to gain meaningful employment suitable to ensure he avoids returning to gaol.

Another service that could have positive impact on an inmate while still incarcerated is to see a psychologist. Regular counselling sessions with a psych might mean that an inmate is able to address some underlying issues which are contributing to him continuing to commit crimes. Many inmates have had traumatic incidents earlier on in their lives. Many of their issues are never resolved, and by seeing a psychologist an inmate may be able to address these previous traumatic life experiences – to bring them to the forefront, address them and learn new coping mechanisms, and then move on with a new life.

Many inmates have a renewed commitment to their various faiths, and this can help them to achieve a new sense of purpose and gravitate away from their previous criminal behaviour. Another very important area that can help an inmate move away from crime is addressing an addiction that has kept them in the cyclic spiral of returning to custody. Gambling, alcohol and drug addictions are an imprisoning way to live whether on the outside or in gaol. If an inmate receives assistance either physically, mentally or both to overcome their addiction, then this can be the key that unlocks that door to freedom, and helps to ensure that they never return to prison again.

STATISTICS OF INCARCERATION AND RECIDIVISM

Examining incarceration rates and recidivism rates around the world

The U.S. releases over 7 million people from gaol each year, however recidivism is common and within three years of their release, 2 out of 3 people are rearrested and more than 50% are incarcerated again.

The U.S. has a recidivism rate of approximately 64%, which means that of the number of people who are released from gaol, 64% return. As defined earlier, they have reverted to their previous criminal behaviour. In contrast to the U.S., Norway has one of the lowest recidivism rates in the world, sitting at around 20%. Australia falls somewhere between these two countries, with a recidivism rate of around 46%. This can move up and down a little but 46% is the national average as of September 2021.

These are very contrasting statistics. In the U.S. around two-thirds of people who are released from gaol will return. Only one in three people do NOT revert to their criminal behaviour. Only one in three people stay out of gaol. By examining the rate of inmates returning to custody in the U.S., it would seem that being imprisoned is not a deterrent to returning to gaol. If a country's only desired outcome is to punish a person for committing a crime, then it would appear that a successful outcome has been achieved. But if a country, or society, aims to achieve something more within its prison system than only punishment, then it would be aiming to have low rates of recidivism within their prison system. There may even be a lesson to be learned by examining these varying statistics on recidivism and incarceration rates.

Australia's prison population

Australia's prison population is increasing in both number and as a proportion of the population.

In the general adult population, prisoners are:

- far more likely to be male—more than 8 in 10 (85%) adult prisoners were male (Australian Institute of Health and Welfare, AIHW 2019).
- more likely to be Aboriginal and Torres Strait Islander
- younger—2 in 3 (66%) prisoners were under 40 (ABS 2018a).

Almost 3 in 4 people entering prison have been in prison before, and almost half (45%) have been in prison within the previous 12 months (AIHW 2019).

Prisoners have higher levels of mental health problems, risky alcohol consumption, tobacco smoking, illicit drug use, chronic disease and communicable diseases than the general population (AIHW 2013). This means they have significant and complex health and welfare needs, often long-term or chronic. The health of prisoners is sufficiently poorer than that of the general community, and prisoners are often considered to be 'old' at age 50–55 (Williams et al. 2014). This poor health is not just physical, either, with the prison population also suffering from inferior mental health to that of the general community. 2 in 5 people entering prison reported a previous diagnosis of a mental health disorder, including alcohol and drug misuse (AIHW 2019).

STATISTICS OF INCARCERATION AND RECIDIVISM

The ability to gain and maintain employment is key to successful reintegration of former prisoners into the community post release. Many prisoners, particularly Indigenous prisoners, have complex and sometimes traumatic personal histories which are not addressed while in prison, and upon their release these issues are a contributing factor to difficulties in gaining employment (COAG 2016).

More than half (54%) of the people entering prison reported that they were unemployed during the 30 days prior to being imprisoned (AIHW 2019).

The majority of prisoners come from a group who already face difficulties in gaining employment. They generally have low levels of education, low socio-economic position, high levels of drug and alcohol misuse, high levels of mental health issues, and poor work histories. When imprisonment is added to this mix, it makes it even more difficult for prisoners to find a job, particularly those who have been in prison for longer than six months (Ramakers et al. 2014).

Fewer than 1 in 4 prisoners discharged from prison reported they had paid employment organised to start within two weeks of their release from prison (AIHW 2019).

A person's education is recognised as a social determinant of health, with lower levels of education associated with poorer health (Mitrou et al. 2014). People in prison have lower levels of educational attainment and higher levels of learning difficulties than people in the general community (AIHW 2015; Kendall & Hopkins 2019). Lower levels of educational attainment are also associated with poorer employment opportunities and outcomes, which is one of the reasons that unemployment is a risk factor for incarceration and for reoffending after release (Baldry et al. 2018).

In 2018, 1 in 3 (33%) prison entrants had not completed Year 10 and 15% had Year 8 or below as their highest level of education completed.

Most (78%) prisoners released from gaol in 2018 were expecting to receive some form of financial assistance from Centrelink. This reliance on income support is yet another difficulty faced by prisoners upon their release.

Unemployment is linked with poor psychosocial outcomes. This includes mental health issues, alcohol and other drug use disorders, and criminal offending (Fergusson et al. 2014).

All of these statistics highlight not only the many contributing factors that are associated with incarceration in Australia, but also the obstacles, which at times seem insurmountable, faced by prisoners when they are released from gaol. It shows the strong correlation between people living with disadvantage, such as lower education and lower opportunities for employment, and entrance into the criminal system, and this is particularly the case for young people.

Aboriginal Australians in prison - Indigenous incarceration

First Nations people of Australia, which includes both Aboriginals and Torres Strait Islanders, are the most incarcerated people on the planet. First Nations people comprise only 3% of our Australian population, but they make up 29% of the adult prison population. Similarly, young First Nations people (Aboriginal and aged 14-24) make up 48% of the youth prison population while they only comprise around 5% of the Australian population of the same age.

It has been said that a First Nations teenage boy is more likely to go to gaol than to university.

A previous statistic states that 54% of people entering into gaol were unemployed, but this statistic increases greatly with Indigenous people entering prison. There is a particularly high level of unemployment amongst Aboriginal prisoners, with 84% of these inmates being unemployed when they were arrested.

There has been an increase in Aboriginals being incarcerated, but the evidence suggests that this increase has occurred because Indigenous offenders are now receiving longer prison sentences. With the possible exception of offences against justice procedures, it does not appear that the increase in imprisonment is due to increased offending (Fitzgerald, 2009).

This chapter has discussed some background information about the rates of incarceration in three different countries. Australia, as a country, shows that it is faring reasonably with recidivism within our country – certainly better than somewhere like the U.S. But these same statistics highlight that we can strive to decrease recidivism rates by implementing principles that have been shown to be beneficial in other parts of the world.

CHAPTER THREE

SUCCESSFUL PRISONS IN SCANDINAVIA AND AUSTRALIA

———————— ◆◇◆ ————————

If Australia wants to reduce its recidivism rates, a good place to start is to look to other countries that are recording low rates in this area.

Norway has one of the lowest rates of recidivism, with around just 20% of prisoners returning to the prison population within three years of being released from prison. At the other end of the spectrum, the U.S. has a recidivism rate of 64%, while Australia sits near the middle at around 46%. What stands out here is that there is a big difference between these numbers and looking at these statistics it seems that Norway is doing something dramatically different to the U.S. that is helping to bring their recidivism rates right down.

And it's not just Norwegian gaols in which this is happening; all Scandinavian prisons have relatively low recidivism rates of around 31%.

Sweden's prison system also boasts impressive numbers. In the past decade, the number of Swedish prisoners has dropped from 5,722 to 4,500 out of a population of 9.5 million. The country has closed a number of prisons, and the recidivism rate is around 40%. This is far less than most European countries, as well as the U.S. as of May, 2016. A major reason for the apparent superiority of Scandinavian prisons is likely that they actually try to educate and rehabilitate their offenders, rather than simply punish them.

It is written that on one occasion, the guards at the Norrtälje prison in Sweden forgot to lock the cell doors of six inmates before changing shifts. Instead of attempting to escape, the men broke into the prison kitchen and baked a chocolate cake, which they ate while watching TV – inside a blanket fort they built.

But it seems that Norway gets the gold star. The offenders in Norwegian gaols are no different to those in the maximum security gaols in Australia. These offenders have been living a fully criminal lifestyle before being incarcerated into Norwegian prisons, and most have been convicted of violent crimes. But it appears that Norway is adopting a policy that no matter how bad their crime is, all the prisoners are treated in a way that gives them a feeling of hope for their future and an opportunity to change their previous criminal behaviour. These offenders do not have to live in the cycle of continuously returning to custody, a cycle which is like a spinning wheel of being released then returning to prison, over and over again.

Norway is known to be one of the safest countries in the world, with extremely low crime rates even in major cities such as Oslo, Bergen, Trondheim and Stavanger. So let's take a closer look at what's happening in Norway by examining two Norwegian gaols in detail.

Halden Prison – Norway

The below paragraphs are excerpts from The Story Institute, which detail the living conditions in Halden prison. The full extract can be found at https://www.thestoryinstitute.com/halden.

Halden is a maximum-security prison. It hosts highly dangerous criminals, including rapists, murderers and child molesters. They compose the majority of the prison population, while a third of the residents are drug offenders.

Halden works off a philosophy that the sentence for the crime is to be locked away from society, rather than enduring hardship every day.

The fact is that these prisoners will eventually be released, and "Who do we want as our neighbour?" These words are almost like a rhetoric slogan or a mantra within the walls of Halden Prison. Even prisoners use these words when talking about the humane conditions of Halden Prison.

Sometimes referred to as the world's most humane prison, Halden Prison does look a bit different to most others. Built in the middle of the woods, the architects wanted to keep as much nature as possible within the prison walls; there are many trees, uneven grounds, blueberries and adders. It would be easy to run and hide, but nobody does.

Inmates live within a communal space. The guards rooms are intentionally designed to be small so that they move out of these rooms and into the inmates' common area. It is very important for security that the guards are out with the inmates for a large part of the time, not sitting in offices.

This campus design has helped these relationships flourish. A study has found that there are few violent and security-related incidents with this campus design.

The cells have a bed, a small fridge, a bookshelf, a TV, a desk and a chair, plus a private bathroom including a shower, toilet and sink. In the school building there is also a grocery store named "Justisen" (The Justice) where inmates can buy whatever they need to cook for themselves and each other. There is also a well-equipped music studio – "Criminal Records" – a garden, a holy room, a gym, training room, library, computer room, family visiting house and more. The school offers prisoners an opportunity to get a proper education while serving their sentence.

During the day, guards often socialise with the prisoners. This can be over waffles and coffee, dinner, volleyball or just casual conversations. Many areas have no surveillance cameras, and prisoners can to some extent move around freely. Some have suggested the prison is too luxurious, and that being in a prison like this is not a proper punishment. Warden Are Høidal (the Governor of Halden Prison) says that revenge alone does not provide any good results. Rehabilitation is key. Finding proper housing and a steady income even before the prisoners are released is believed to contribute to lower recidivism rates.

The architecture of Halden Prison has been designed to minimise residents' sense of incarceration, to ease psychological stress and to put them in harmony with the surrounding nature – in fact, the prison has won several design awards for its minimalist chic.

Halden's architects preserved trees across the 75-acre site to obscure the 20-foot-high security wall that surround the perimeter, in order to minimise the institutional feel and, in the words of one architect, to "let the inmates see all of the seasons". Benches and stone chessboards dot a jogging trail which follows the perimeter of the prison.

The prison's exterior features earthy brown hues which help it to blend in with the surrounding woodlands. Inside, however, the walls explode with colour. Halden hired an interior decorator who used 18 different colours to create a sense of variety and stimulate various moods. A calming shade of green creates a soothing atmosphere in the cells, while a vivid orange brings energy to the library and other working areas. There is a two-bedroom guesthouse, where inmates can host their families overnight, and which includes a conjugal room painted a fiery red.

The maximum sentence in Norway, even for murder, is 21 years. Since most inmates will eventually return to society, prisons mimic the outside world as much as possible to prepare them for freedom. At Halden, rooms include en-suite bathrooms with ceramic tiles, mini-fridges and flat-screen TVs. Officials say sleeker televisions afford inmates less space to hide drugs and other contraband.

RETRIBUTION OR REHABILITATION

Every 10 to 12 cells share a kitchen and living room, where prisoners prepare their evening meals and relax after a day of work. None of the windows at Halden have bars.

Security guards organise activities from 8:00 in the morning until 8:00 in the evening. It's a chance for inmates to pick up a new hobby, but it's also a part of the prison's dynamic security strategy: occupied prisoners are less likely to lash out at guards and one another. Inmates can shoot hoops on this basketball court, which absorbs falls on impact, and make use of a rock-climbing wall, jogging trails and a soccer field.

There's also a recording studio with a professional mixing board. In-house music teachers — who refer to the inmates as "pupils," never "prisoners" — work with their charges on piano, guitar, bongos and more.

Norway's prison guards undergo two years of training at an officers' academy and enjoy an elevated status compared with their peers in the U.S. and Britain. Their official job description says they must motivate the inmate "so that his sentence is as meaningful, enlightening and rehabilitating as possible," so they frequently eat meals and play sports with prisoners. At Halden, half of all guards are female, which its governor believes reduces tension and encourages good behaviour.

To help inmates develop routines and to reduce the monotony of confinement, designers spread Halden's living quarters, work areas and activity centres across the prison grounds. There is a "kitchen laboratory," where inmates learn the basics of nutrition and cooking. On any afternoon, homemade orange sorbet and slices of tropical fruit that line a table can be seen. Prisoners can take courses that will prepare them for careers as caterers, chefs and waiters.

No inmate has ever tried to escape from Halden Prison.

Bastøy Prison, Norway

The following few paragraphs are excerpts from an article found at allthatsinteresting.com/bastoy-prison, which details Bastøy prison and also includes comments from Arne Kvernik-Nilsen, the founding Governor of Bastøy Prison.

Bastøy Prison is a minimum-security prison on Bastøy Island, Norway. The prison is on a 2.6-square kilometre island and hosts 115 inmates. Arne Kvernvik-Nilsen, former governor of the prison, leads a staff of 69 prison employees.

It has been called "the Norwegian prison that works" by *The Guardian* and "the world's nicest prison" by *CNN*. At Bastøy Prison, inmates live communally in comfortable homes. Each man has his own room and shares the kitchen and other facilities with the other inmates. A meal a day is provided for them; any other food must be bought from the local supermarket and prepared by the prisoners themselves, who receive an allowance of $90 a month.

The inmates also earn roughly eight dollars a day on a variety of jobs that include growing food, looking after horses, repairing bicycles, doing woodwork, and maintaining Bastøy Island's facilities. Every inmate is offered high-quality education and training programs to increase their skills.

The prison is on an island one square mile in size and hosts 115 inmates with a staff of 69 prison employees. Only five employees remain on the island overnight.

In their free time, inmates have the opportunity to visit the church, school, or library, and engage in leisure activities such as horse riding, fishing, and tennis. All the guards have received three years' training (compared to perhaps six months in the US), and resemble social workers more than prison officers.

"It is not just because Bastøy is a nice place, a pretty island to serve prison time, that people change," Arne Kvernvik Nilsen, Warden, the founding Governor of Bastøy Prison. "The staff here are very important. They are like social workers as well as prison guards. They believe in their work and know the difference they are making."

Nilsen has revolutionary thoughts about how prisons should be run. He also acknowledges the difficulties that the public faces in rethinking how prisoners should be treated. Nilsen stated:

"If someone did very serious harm to one of my daughters or my family... I would probably want to kill them. That's my reaction. But as a prison governor or politician, we have to approach this in a different way. We have to respect people's need for revenge, but not use that as a foundation for how we run our prisons... Should I be in charge of adding more problems to the prisoner on behalf of the state, making you an even worse threat to larger society because I have treated you badly while you are in my care? We know that prison harms people. I look at this place as a place of healing, not just of your social wounds but of the wounds inflicted on you by the state in your four or five years in eight square meters of high security."

As of 2014, Norway's incarceration rate was at only 75 per 100,000 people. In addition, since developing its new prison system in the 1990s, its recidivism rate has decreased from around 60-70% to only 20% in recent years (6 Jan, 2021).

Macquarie Correctional Centre, Wellington NSW – Corrective Services NSW

Macquarie Correctional Centre seems to run as a therapeutic community. I am not sure if this was initially intended but since it began operating in December 2017 it has taken on this persona. I examine therapeutic communities operating inside prisons more in the following chapter.

Macquarie Correctional Centre employs the philosophy that any person, at any age, can be rehabilitated. They aim to break the cycle of former inmates continuously returning to custody, and instead attempt to teach them to become meaningful members of society. So how is that done at Macquarie CC? To begin, the inmates are housed in dormitories with 25 inmates in each rather than living in a cell.

I feel that most of us would understand that when we live in society, we do not live in cells, isolated from other people. In society we live as a community, often with many people living together. Living as a community teaches us skills. When you lock a person up in a cell, they do not have to develop those same skills. Those skills include learning to be tolerant of other people, and being tolerant of different situations that may be challenging. These might include situations where there are rooms full of people that they don't really like, or they may be noisy or threatening situations. If a person learns to tolerate these situations, at the same time they are learning how to be more resilient. They learn social skills like how to react in a socially acceptable manner. If someone is annoying, you don't have to react verbally or physically by abusing them – you can learn to be tolerant.

The inmates at Macquarie CC interact with prison staff on a frequent basis. These staff members can model socially acceptable behavior for incarcerated inmates who may have never previously had good role models in their life. The prison staff speak to the inmates in a respectful manner. It is very important that the correctional officers are trained to speak to the inmates in this way. When people are treated respectfully, they usually mirror this same behaviour.

The officers have contact with the inmates on multiple occasions throughout the day, and so they learn to use every interaction as a training opportunity. There was a program introduced into NSW gaols recently which is modelled off a similar program that has been successful in the U.K. It is about all prison staff, but correctional officers in particular, having constructive conversations with inmates and using every interaction as a learning opportunity for the inmate.

Often correctional officers will be heard complimenting an inmate for a job that they have done well. This might be a good weld in the engineering workshop, a good result from an assignment they have submitted or a good presentation speech at Toastmasters. They've done a good job, whether it's working, whether it's at a speaking event, or whether it's to do with helping a correctional officer – or even one of their fellow inmates – with cleaning or something similar.

There's a strong connection between the way the prison staff interact and treat the inmates, and the resulting behaviour that the inmates display. This is just one of many of the contributing factors within a gaol that is modelled off a therapeutic community.

Within the gaol the inmates are also given constructive activities daily. This means that they are not just sitting around getting bored all day. They have meaningful, purposeful days where they learn things such as mechanical skills, information about their Indigenous culture, or a range of workplace skills that they can take back out into the workplace which will enable them to contribute to society. All these factors help to establish the idea that they're doing a job that's worthwhile, and that they are respected for it. Everyone likes to be appreciated – it makes you feel good inside and raises your self-esteem, and inmates are no different.

CHAPTER FOUR

GAOLS AS A THERAPEUTIC COMMUNITY

◆◇◆

The main resource used for this chapter is: Offender Rehabilitation and Therapeutic Communities – Enabling Change the TC Way by Alisa Stevens, 2012.

In this chapter I will closely examine the idea that therapeutic communities in gaols are vehicles to stimulate and support the change of a criminal into a person who can lead a meaningful and productive life after their release from gaol. Although some of the resource information can be a little heavy, I do urge you to hang in there and absorb this data, because it gives strength to the idea that therapeutic communities within gaol walls can be valuable vehicles to an inmate's rehabilitation.

RETRIBUTION OR REHABILITATION

The following is an extract from Alisa Stevens' book: "A therapeutic community is a treatment model which allows an individual, often a troubled person, to attend and be part of a social community. The aim of a therapeutic community is, over time, to help the resident overcome their social and emotional problems. This is done in two ways. The first of these is through residents actively participating in group therapy in order to unearth, examine and work through their often unconscious motives, unresolved conflicts, and learned maladaptive self-protective behaviours that can result from traumatic or abusive formative experiences (Mellon 1979, Cordless and Williams 1996, Camplin 2001). The second is through residents' contribution to the daily nurturance of an interdependent, cohesive, pro-social environment, including involvement in specific activities of therapeutic benefit to the individual and of practical and domestic benefit to other community members.

An important part of the therapeutic community is that the residents have input into the running of the place. When constructing prisons which will follow the therapeutic community model, there needs to be consideration of building institutions which are not solely focused on locking people up and keeping the community safe, an ideology which is implemented at the expense of the inmates it houses. Inmates in a typical gaol are not seen for their individual personalities."

People are social beings and like to contribute to the community that they live in. So, in a therapeutic community, the residents within that institution are actively contributing to their own process of desistance and change. They need to feel that their decisions and opinions are valued and that they are worthwhile people. They not only need to have input into the running of the place, but they also have to work hard on themselves while being a member of that community.

The therapeutic community, as an instrument, provides daily "living, learning experiences", opportunities for self-discovery and important "two-way communication of content and feeling, listening, interaction, and problem-solving, leading to learning" (Jones, 1980). Over time, the residents learn to reflect upon and understand their problems and work through these towards change. There is a general "feel" in a therapeutic community of a dynamic culture where every incident, every interaction is potentially a subject for therapeutic scrutiny. Each member of the community should be able to participate equally in the administrative decision-making and contribute meaningfully to other residents' therapy. This allows residents to acquire a profound sense of investment in, ownership of, and responsibility to their community's decisions, their implications and implementation, and the safe and effective functioning of the community.

Within a therapeutic community there is the doctrine that all people are equal and deserve equal rights and opportunities. Therefore, all the amenities within the facility as well as domestic arrangements are shared between residents and staff on an informal basis. The residents' mistakes are accepted rather than being condemned. Periodically, however, the residents will receive constructive "therapeutic feedback", in which community members relate the impact such behaviour has upon them.

In prisons, the therapeutic community represents a counter-culture – a different form of imprisonment and offender rehabilitation. For prisoners, this means the therapeutic community seeks to resist the "criminalistic ideology" (Clemmer, 1958). Criminalistic ideology can best be described as a basic concept of punishment. So, within the walls of prisons that are adopting the therapeutic community model, there must be a relinquishment of some of the decision-making to the inmates. This is a difficult concept to adopt in a maximum-security gaol, where historically the focus has been on maintaining security.

The therapeutic community model within a prison as a method of offender rehabilitation seems to defy the established idea of managing risk of harm and re-offending to instead offer help to the offender as a whole person, with complex, multi-dimensional needs. These people often have low self-esteem and very minimal aspirations and expectations for a productive and peaceful life after their release from prison. The aim of the therapeutic community within a prison setting is to ensure that the community member (inmate) can enjoy a "stable life in a real role in the real world" once they have left the therapeutic community (Main, 1996). As a result, the living experience within the community needs to be as "normal" as possible, so that it can offer daily opportunities to acquire and practice "normal" ways of being, behaving, and relating to and interacting with others.

In her book *Offender Rehabilitation and Therapeutic Communities – Enabling Change the TC Way,* author Alyssa Stevens argues that what helps to promote positive change is the development of a more adaptive and perceptive self-narrative, combined with an improved concept of oneself (which is no longer compatible with serious offending). Inmates have this new "identity reconstruction" which becomes possible because of the ways in which therapeutic communities provide opportunities for their "residents" to live within a community which reinforces different moral codes (of conduct, values and culture) and which allows for the emergence of a new person, a new identity. They would describe this as a "new me". This new identity is accepted and valued by their peers, and helps to reinforce and reaffirm the possibility and "achievability" of change. According to Stevens, "residents within therapeutic communities therefore enjoy a shared social identity; namely members of a superior 'penal club' who are consciously and actively, to varying degrees, trying to change".

While living within a therapeutic community, the member needs to go through a period of change – an evolving identity change. Therapeutic communities tend to encourage and foster positive resistance-focused identity, like a reconstruction of the person, which means that the old way of thinking of the original person evolves into that of a new person. That new person has new values and new morals that align with most social norms. This process of the emergence of a new person occurs over time. As this new person emerges, their ideas are to resist against that criminalistic ideology, against the inmate code. The inmate code to which I refer can best be defined as: a set of rules and values that have developed among prisoners inside prisons' social systems. This inmate code emphasises unity of prisoners against "the system" (which combines police, correctional centres and their staff and any form of law enforcement). The inmates band together and act united against the system. This inmate code is very thick and strong.

To look more closely at the process of desistance, I will use the analogy of an onion. As this process evolves, it is similar to an onion. The idea of changing a person's identity from one thing into another is, understandably, a very long process. There are many layers to be peeled back, and exposing each layer to the elements can be a slow and painful experience for the person. Along this journey, they need to address many of their underlying issues that have led them to the criminal lifestyle that they have been recently living. Post trauma from their childhood, issues of neglect and abuse are exposed and have to be dealt with individually before this person can move on and peel off another layer. What lies at the core of this onion is their true self, and the realisation of the person that they want to be in their new future life. This person then needs encouragement and a raising of their self-worth, their self-esteem. They need to know that they really do deserve a better life than that which they had been living before coming to gaol. The initial motivation to change has to come from that person. They need to say, "I want help. I want to change."

This is a really important, pivotal point. I think we all know that if a person is forced into something that they do not want to do themselves, then it is not going to be successful. If you said to a person, "Right, I've decided that you should give up tobacco smoking" – do you think that would work? Particularly if that same person responds with "I don't want to stop smoking". I do not think that anyone would believe that would work.

Changing a person's identity is exactly the same, if not even more so, because being a cigarette smoker is just a slice of that person's traits and only part of their life, while being a criminal is a whole lifestyle. An entirely new person must be created. It is like the birth of a new person. Recently an inmate, who had undergone this process, on his release day said to me that "Last time I was released (from gaol) you (the correctives system) were releasing an animal...this time you are releasing a man".

This is because that new man has started to emerge. He was evolving, becoming a new character. The man was starting to see that the idea of a new person was strong in him. There was this awareness within him, and the entire gaol hierarchy and staff were behind him, saying "We believe in you". We (the system) believe that you can really change and become the man that you want to be.

Humans are social beings. We draw together for connection and friendship. Prisoners are no exception to that. They are social. So that idea of banding together, that cohesiveness, that "It's us against them" mindset, is nearly like a gang mentality. It is hard in gaol to step forward and be an individual. It is hard for an inmate to move away from that INMATE CODE and say, "No, I don't agree with that. I disagree that idea." Because that inmate code is thick and strong. It takes a lot of strength on that individual's behalf to go against that code. In order to develop a new identity, that individual inmate has had to move himself away from that mentality, and realise within himself that he is capable of making his own decisions and then acting upon them with conviction and determination.

The basic, most fundamental level of the therapeutic community model is that prisoners are treated with decency. The communication between prison officers and inmates is very important. The way these officers speak to the inmates, the way they interact, needs to be one of common decency. In a prison environment that is operating as a therapeutic community, the idea of offender rehabilitation for that prison has to go beyond just minimising risk of harm or re-offending. It is not totally focused on the upholding of security, although this does still need to be a large consideration. It has to be optimistic and believe that the community members are capable of change – that the prison is helping them to rehabilitate and evolve into that new identity of a person who is not a criminal. It is helping them reach their own individual potential. The member will be able to view themselves differently and have renewed aspirations for a life that they once thought was unachievable. To believe they are capable of maintaining and living a stable, happy life. As an inmate moves through that process of change, forensic therapeutic communities have the potential to motivate a seriously violent offender and help them to evolve into the best person that they can be.

We have been looking at the idea of a person progressing through a therapeutic community. At the end of that process, or the end of their sentence, we are now looking at a new person. They have had an identity reconstruction, and the new person now views themselves as someone who can contribute to society, instead of taking away from it (as they had done in their former life).

In the prison environment, I am a firm believer that therapeutic communities can be valuable instruments in the process of change.

CHAPTER FIVE

MOTIVATING CHANGE IN CURRENT AND FORMER OFFENDERS

———— ◆◇◆ ————

In this chapter, we are going to look at what motivates a criminal to change their lifestyle – to refrain from their current criminal behaviour and become a law-abiding citizen. In previous chapters I have discussed the concept of change as a criminal metamorphosing into a whole new person, to the point that they no longer identify with the person that they used to be. Now, I am going to examine what motivates somebody to want to change.

When a person earns money illegally it is often called dirty money. It comes in easily and goes out easily. Ten thousand dollars could be earnt and gone in the same day. This is money that is made through criminal activity, which may be from something like a break and enter or selling drugs. This money is seen as dirty money and is consequently spent on dirty things such as buying drugs, prostitutes or gambling. It's easy come, easy go. A person caught up in a criminal lifestyle can make a lot of money quickly, only to spend it straight away and, in no time at all, have nothing to show for the money they had previously made.

Dirty money is spent that same way that it comes in – on dirty things. In contrast, when money is made legally, it's called clean money. This money comes from working hard to earn it, then saving it like a hard-working citizen for a better future. It's subsequently spent on things that are clean – on legal rather than stolen goods. This might be something for that person's mother. It might be something that they've longed for. And, since they've worked hard for that money, there is a sense of accomplishment and satisfaction from spending it legally. This is a very interesting difference – that when you work hard and save money there's a lot more thought and decision going into what to use it on. In contrast, dirty money comes in quickly and goes out just as quickly. It is like it just slips through your hands.

So, if an offender can earn a lot of money illegally, then why would he make a conscious choice to earn less money, even if that money would be clean and something that he has legally earned. What would be the motivator to do that? Could the motivator be self-esteem? That he wants to feel better about himself? By making clean money, could it be that he would feel a lot better within himself? Could the motivator be that he doesn't want to lead this lifestyle anymore? Maybe the motivators are his children. Often an inmate will be thinking that he would like to be a better role model for his kids. He might be motivated to be a better role model to his children than his own parents have been for him. He may want to bring his children up the legal, clean way, so that his children's lives don't evolve into a similar one to what he has been living.

When the offender is caught up in the cycle of making dirty money and spending dirty money, he feels like he has lost control of his life. He might feel like he is a hamster on a spinning wheel, going around and around. That he isn't driving this machine but it is driving him. This offender may look inside himself and say, "Do I respect this person that I have become? Do I want this child of mine to have to lead this same life that I have? I want to get back in the driver's seat and take control of my own life. This criminal life that I have been living is a highly stressful one, and I am always looking over my shoulder. I am burdened by anxiety and conflicts with police."

The core of this comes down to self-respect and the idea of his own self-esteem. There is this motivating force that he wants to be a better person. That he wants to feel better about himself. He wants to be able to look other community members in the eye, look his children in the eye, look his mother in the eye and say, "I earned this money. I worked hard for it, and I feel good about myself."

An inmate's life is one of isolation because they are locked away from society. Away from their families and all the people who they care about, and who care about them. When life keeps chugging along on the outside, it is doing so without them being a part of it. Significant events in the family often take place while they are in gaol. Weddings, christenings, birthdays all happen without them. But a really important event that can happen while an inmate is incarcerated is the death of someone important if their life. I knew a young inmate whose father had become terminally ill while he was incarcerated. He talked about how deeply this had affected him. That he was not able to ever see his father again, and he was not able to attend his funeral. He felt he had let his mother down, saying that he was not there for his mother. He was not able to support his mother through the process of his father dying. This motivated him to be a better son to his mother, to help support her emotionally when he was released from gaol.

There is a range of motivating forces that can contribute to an inmate wanting to change their criminal behaviour, to change their life. But it's important that they are the person who makes that decision, and that they are prepared to work hard at this process of change. If they decide that they don't want to live that same criminal life, they need to be very aware that they have to totally change their lifestyle, not just a small part of it.

When they are in gaol, these people are isolated from their peers and the gangs that might have influenced them to walk down the path of crime. The inmate is very aware that these associates were a significant factor of their criminal behaviour. This inmate becomes aware that he would like to change and comes to the realisation that there is a lot of really hard work to do. Fortunately, gaol can be the ideal place to begin this work as they are away from these associates, and are able to focus on their rehabilitation. They can work in industries learning new skills. They can work on themselves and adjust their way of thinking. The inmate does not have the distraction of those negative influences. This inmate is thinking, "I do not want to return to gaol, I am strong and determined to reject those people". Their mind has changed, they have changed their persona.

But although they have changed while they have been on the inside, the outside world has not changed. If this inmate returns to that same criminal environment, it is very hard for them to resist the temptations that they will be surrounded by. All of a sudden they are back with their mates, returning to the same lifestyle that brought them to gaol in the first place. This newly released inmate is now confronted with a wall of obstacles, and it can be an overwhelming situation. The resistance and determination he thought that he had on the inside is being undermined and he can see that the new life that he was envisaging for himself is now slowly melting away. It takes an enormous amount of effort to resist these obstacles, and is a lot easier to just slide back into that same lifestyle. Choosing the alternate path is much harder, but it is also much more rewarding. It means that that this former inmate gets a lot more satisfaction. It gives him a raised sense of esteem. He can hold his head up high. He has a newfound pride in this new achievement. He can now be a respected community member. When he was leading a criminal lifestyle, he was looked upon by the community as scum, and he felt a sense of awkwardness. Gaining respect from other people is often a significant motivator to change.

A person's self-perception is a big part of who they are. It defines how that person sees themselves, and can vary significantly from person to person. "I'm just a crim and will never amount to anything else." "I can achieve my goal as long as I stay focused." "I am an approachable person who is firm but fair." "I'm just a junkie." If a person examines themselves closely and doesn't like what they see, then they may decide that they want to do something about themselves. This might be something as simple as going to dance classes.

When an inmate examines themselves their question might be, "Do I want to continue to live this life?" Many inmates get caught up in that never-ending cycle of being incarcerated, doing time, being released, committing more crime, being out on parole, evoking an intensive community corrections order, having their parole revoked and then returning to custody. This culminates in spending more time in gaol. It is just a cycle, a wheel turning around and around. I often think it resembles one of those mice running on a wheel just going around and around.

Some inmates eventually start to question this revolving life at a certain point, and this point is often known as criminal menopause. This typically occurs in their mid-forties. People experiencing criminal menopause have been in and out of gaol basically all their adult life, since they were 18 years of age. Many inmates have been involved with the legal system even prior to entering into adult custody, having spent time in juvenile justice as kids or boys' detention homes. They have been involved in that whole cycle of criminality and contact with the law not only all their adult life, but for much of their juvenile life as well. So maybe after many years of that, they start to question whether this is the life they want to continue with. At this stage they might think about making changes, or alternatively they may not be able to envisage another life because this way of living is all they have ever known, and they can't even see that they could obtain a different type of life. For others, however, there is a strong motivating force that poses the question, "Do I want to continue on the same hamster wheel or do I want to take a different path which is going to be initially a lot of hard work?"

So, as we look along this idea of change, what are some of the different factors that might motivate a person to change?

Even among those who are motivated to change, however, some can't link that with the physical activity of actually doing it. I think we can all relate to that. It is a lot easier to think about doing something than it is to actually do it. One of the physical actions could be included within this process of change might be kicking a drug habit, something which is an enormous obstacle just within itself. Kicking that drug habit might mean attending residential rehab.

Another physical action could be getting skills to go to work. Many inmates have not worked at all, or at least not much, and if they have they often don't have many work skills. They often don't have those employability skills. This inmate may think, "What am I going to get a job doing? I want a job that earns good money, but I don't have any skills." This may mean that the physical effort is acquiring some skills, learning to become a bricky or concreter. Acquiring these skills might involve getting some training at TAFE or on a building site and talking to employers. It requires a lot of hard work and determination.

While they are in custody, inmates feel as if their life is standing still while other people's lives are continue on. When they enter gaol, it is like the pause button has been pushed while their friends' lives are still on play. While they are incarcerated, their friends get married, start new jobs, go on holidays and buy themselves houses. All this time the inmate does none of these things – they are just sitting in gaol waiting to resume their life once they are released from custody. When they entered gaol some of their friends might have been apprentice tradesman, but those same friends are no longer working for a boss – they have gone out on their own and started up their own business. They have worked their way up and they might have even started to employ other people. But when that inmate gets released, they feel that they are still stuck years in the past. Their mates have moved on, their lives have progressed, while that of the inmate has stood still.

Even with the best intentions to change, some offenders feel stuck, stranded and are often unable to make that change of lifestyle a reality. So what keeps them stuck? Maybe it is the fact that it is just too hard. It is too hard to change old habits. Too hard to leave all the ties of your old life and start a new one. There may be too many roadblocks, too many walls to climb over, that make it too difficult to get to the other side. As a result, they just remain in that criminal lifestyle and never change.

I think all of us are quite aware that, as human beings, we don't like change. Whether it's changing house, changing jobs; we love that warm, soft, familiar comfort of things being the same. It's comforting. Our own security blanket. If someone is self-motivated, self-driven and employs self-talk about pushing themselves out of their comfort zone, that's when change can happen, but to create movement and momentum you've got to push forward. It is human nature not to like change because when you're comfortable, it's just so easy to keep doing the same thing. So some inmates do just remain stuck. Stuck in a rut. They can't get off that spinning wheel because there are just too many impediments to change. They can't envisage themselves as that other person, that person with a new identity. And so, that criminal cycle continues.

✦ ✦ ✦

CHAPTER SIX

DIFFERENT FORMS OF REHABILITATION

◆◇◆

In this chapter, I am going to look at different forms of rehabilitation. In Chapter Four, I discussed the model of setting up therapeutic communities within the confines of a prison, while in this chapter we are going to examine the range of different options that are available for rehabilitation.

An important part of the change of identity for the member of the gaol community which we have previously discussed starts in an inmate's mind while he is still in gaol. The process of rehabilitation has been shown to begin long before a person is released from prison.

The effective relationships that are developed between officers and residents was highlighted as a very significant factor in the success of the Norwegian gaols discussed in Chapter Three. These relationships help to develop a trust between officers and residents, and this trust results in clear communication between the correctional officers and the inmates that are in their charge within the gaol. The purposeful conversations are designed to shift the residents' thinking towards change.

Five-minute interventions is a program that uses every opportunity that an officer has with an inmate as a learning or coaching opportunity. An inmate builds up a relationship with a particular officer who he knows he can go to if he has a problem, needs something done for him or just to have a chat.

These opportunities that a correctional officer has with inmates can be in many different areas. They could arise when walking down with him to the clinic, in a workshop, or anytime throughout the day when an officer has contact with an inmate – all of these instances are seen as opportunities to have a positive experience for the inmate, a learning experience. Those five-minute interventions are a conversation with an officer which might help to trigger something. It might be, "Have you spoken to your family lately?" or, "Is there something that I can help you with?" Then the inmate might reply with, "Well, actually I do have a problem", "You could help me with...." or, "Could you help me with reconnecting with my family, because I have been estranged from them for a long time".

The relationship continually builds between the inmate and the correctional officer over time. Inmates often don't trust many people at all. They often don't even trust their closest friends and

DIFFERENT FORMS OF REHABILITATION

family, let alone a correctional officer who is basically acting as the reinforcer of the law. But if one day the inmate has a really big problem, it's beneficial if he has built up some trust with an officer, because it means he will be able to go to that officer for help. During these interactions, the inmate and correctional officer start to build a little bit of relationship. This further reinforces that when that inmate needs something, he can go to that particular officer. The inmate may begin a conversation with the officer that starts with something like, "Since I spoke to you six weeks ago, I contacted my family and now I have been speaking to them regularly. I am now much more engaged with family. This makes me feel a lot happier, because it has been something that has been on my mind and eating at me for a long time now." So, this interaction between the inmate and officer has been a positive experience. The inmate might then view that officer in a more positive way, which means that he is a lot more likely to go back to that officer in the future.

The other great thing that comes out of these interactions is that they reduce the tensions between officers and inmates. That inmate code is broken down a little. This makes the whole prison environment a safer place for everyone. Research suggests that this connection between inmates and staff reduces assaults on officers by inmates, which makes sense because, if we think of it from our own perspectives, would you want to harm someone who you trust, who you rely on to help you, someone who you have built a positive connection with? I think that most of us would comfortably say that the answer to this question is "no".

The way that the officers speak to the inmates is an important factor in these relationships. Again, if we put ourselves into this situation – if someone spoke to you disrespectfully and were rude, how would you respond back to them? In contrast, if you were spoken to in a respectful manner, your response is likely to be quite different. This is the same for the inmates and they respond appropriately when addressed with respect and dignity.

This communication between officer and inmates is another piece added to the puzzle that contributes to an inmate actively becoming a more responsible, rational human being.

So, the first part of this inmate/officer communication is to ensure that there's a feeling of trust built between the inmate and an officer. The second relates to how inmates are spoken to – if they are spoken to in a respectful manner, they will likely mirror this back. Both of these factors contribute to a safer environment for everyone within the gaol walls.

There is also a third component to this process, and that is that these quick conversations can be used as learning activities for the inmate to think about his actions and the resulting consequence, reassess them, and then learn from them and maybe choose a different way to response if a similar situation arises in the future. This may arise through thought-provoking questions that the officer may ask while with the inmate for a brief period, like when escorting them to the clinic.

The conversation might go something like this:

Inmate: I would really like to talk to my sister. Her and I used to be pretty close, she's always helped me a lot. And she would be a good person for me to bounce ideas off. But you know, we haven't spoken for years. And last time we did, she told me that she never wanted me to speak to her again, and that I only made her life harder.

DIFFERENT FORMS OF REHABILITATION

Officer: Why do you think your sister thinks like that? Has there been anything in the past that you think might have led her say something like that?

Inmate: Yeah, well when I was renting accommodation through Housing New South Wales, I was on the run. I knew the police were after me. So, I took off and just left the place, left it abandoned. I didn't contact anyone, not even New South Wales Housing. These mates of mine had come around and got really rowdy and trashed the place. Housing contacted my sister because she was down as my next of kin. And then she had to actually arrange for all the stuff to get collected out of the property, get the place fixed up after my crappy mates had trashed it and she also had to pay some unpaid rent. I haven't thought about it much but I reckon that was a pretty crappy situation that I left her in.

Officer: How would you feel if that happened to you? Can you understand why your sister might think like that? Has she ever been dumped into a similar situation like that before?

I'm not on shift for the next few days, but I'll be back on Monday. Why don't we catch up after lunch musters on Monday and see how things are going for you?

Through this conversation, the officer has planted a few seeds, and afterwards the inmate will have a few days to think about it. Over the next few days, the inmate might think of all the problems that he may have caused for his sister. Those seeds that the officer planted begin to grow into an idea.

Hopefully, the inmate will start to think about these things and then let that idea settle. He will have a little bit of space and time to process that information. Then when they meet a few days later, the inmate has been thinking about the questions that the officer had asked him.

Officer: How do you think that you could make contact with your sister or make amends? Have you got some ideas that you think could help?

So again, more questions are asked. The initial seed was planted in the first conversation, and then continues getting watered each time they talk. That water settles and sinks in, then that seed sprouts, then gets a little more water. It keeps growing and growing. And that one small seed could grow into a big plant, and this plant is the ideas and actions that the inmate takes. The officer acts as a mentor, helping and guiding the inmate, giving him encouragement and guidance so that he is able come up with solutions to solve his own problems.

Once inmates are released, rehabilitation and support services are also set up to help them move out of incarceration and assist in making the quantum leap into becoming a functioning a community member. The joining of services helps to contribute to a released offender transitioning into society. These different services link together, creating a safety net of support around the inmate, all working in partnership to ensure the inmate's successful transition.

Some residential drug and alcohol rehabilitation centres offer outreach programs for people who live in isolated areas. We all know that a lot of incarcerated people are Indigenous and they often live in outback, isolated communities. If a person is either released from custody or there is a court order, they must

DIFFERENT FORMS OF REHABILITATION

attend an Alcohol and Other Drugs (AOD) rehab centre. The rehabilitation programs vary in length but are often around three months. When the client has finished the program, the outreach system keeps in contact with that person. For the 90 days during which that client was at the residential rehab, they had been under a really close, intensive situation, often attending daily counselling sessions, and having different interventions daily. Having an outreach team is a way to keep in contact with that person and catch up with them regularly, giving them support and advice, because it's been shown that this ongoing support can be critical when a person is at a tipping point. That contact at the right time might help that person to reach out if they're in a desperate need. They might be able to ring or contact that outreach community team in another way. These teams not only keep in contact with clients over the phone but they also travel around the state supporting their clients.

A workplace is important as well. Being able to get a stable job when leaving gaol is a crucial factor in ensuring that person is able to stay out of gaol in the future. One system which exists to aid inmates in finding a job once they are released is the development of employable skills which some industries in gaols provide them. There are a wide range of industries involved in this. The different types of industries include areas like building relocatable housing, where skills of carpentry and joinery are developed. Another industry which upskills inmates prior to their release is in forest regions, with inmates working in the sawmills, while the engineering industry teaches them metal fabrication skills and welded products are produced. In these workshops, welded goods are produced for both internal and external clients.

Other industries which teach the inmates employment skills include laundry, kitchen and seaming fabrics. In the sewing area, items like sheets and towels are made and repairs are done, while in the kitchen department, inmates learn how to prepare food, which is usually accompanied by a food hygiene course to give them a theoretical knowledge on storage temperatures of food and the associated dangerous bacteria growth that can result if these hygiene routines are not followed.

There are also carpentry workshops where timber products are produced. These products include items such as desks, cabinets and also smaller community products like those cute little boxes for street libraries.

The time spent within these industries enables the inmates to gain practical skills, but they are particularly valuable when they are followed up with qualifications to do with that industry. If an inmate is working in a carpentry workshop and can get a carpentry traineeship, then this significantly improves their chance of employment. If the valuable practical skills they gain from the workshop can be accompanied by a nationally recognised certificate in carpentry or joinery, then it obviously makes them more employable when they leave gaol.

Another important part of rehabilitation is the idea of helping others. There is a theory in therapeutic communities that if person A helps person B, then person A gets better. So, this idea of mentoring and helping is a really positive experience for both parties, in particular the person who is acting as the mentor. I know that a similar train of thought is worked through with AA (Alcoholics Anonymous). A client at AA who is travelling well through the program and has benefited from the AA philosophy

DIFFERENT FORMS OF REHABILITATION

might be asked to work as a sponsor to a newer member of the AA community. We all know the wonderful feeling we get when we help someone else. This same idea is carried through onto a much larger scale. When we help someone else, we feel that we have received more than we have given. So that similar concept can be used with rehabilitation as well.

A person who has been in a similar experience recently is often the best person to help others in a similar situation. So, the best mentors for newly released inmates are inmates who have made the successful transition from custody to community themselves. Newly released inmates need a lot of support, and who better to help support them than someone who has recently done a similar thing? The mentor will have experienced that same anxiety of being in areas where there are large numbers of people, like supermarkets. They will have felt alone out in the community, which is in contrast to custody where you were surrounded be fellow inmates. They will know how hard it is to secure permanent appropriate housing. They will know how hard it is reporting to parole when you are trying hard to work at a job, hoping that your new boss can see the potential in you.

The sponsee (newly released inmate) feels a connection to the mentor because they can relate to what the mentor is saying. They feel that the mentor genuinely knows what they are talking about because they have already walked the same path that the sponsee is walking right now.

In the same vein, a drug addict who has recently been abstaining from illicit drugs, who has been clean, makes a fantastic drug and alcohol counsellor in the future because they have walked the same road and know the pitfalls that are waiting around every corner. I also think that this experience helps the mentor to detect when the other person is avoiding a problem, putting up barriers, blaming other people for their circumstances. The mentor can really call them out on because they can easily relate to these same defense mechanisms that they were using not very long ago.

There becomes a good, developed relationship, a special bond, because the person who needs help can really see that the person helping them is genuine. But why is it that person who is acting as the mentor is going to get better – why would that be? Put simply, it's because they have a sense of purpose. It raises their self-esteem and begins to have a snowballing effect. The more confident they feel, the more their self-esteem rises. They then feel more confident still, as well as more capable, because they are extending their skills.

But not only in the area in which they're acting as a mentor – they might become better public citizens. They might want to then devote some of their own time to other community projects, maybe working in a volunteer community like a soup kitchen, giving food to the homeless. That whole feeling of self-worth, that improved self-image, then helps them, the mentor, to become better within themselves. So, that idea of helping each other gets bigger and better. The mentor receives benefit from their efforts that they contribute, while the sponsee receives the benefits of getting advice and guidance from someone who has recently achieved a similar thing to what they are trying to do right now. It is a really strong basis for getting ex-criminals, or reformed drug addicts, to mentor and help their fellow offenders along that process and road of change into a better life in the future.

✦ ✦ ✦

CHAPTER SEVEN

THE INTERVIEW

———— ◆◇◆ ————

During the writing of this book, I was fortunate enough to have the chance to interview a man recently released from custody. This chapter includes what he described to me in our conversation.

This man was incarcerated at Macquarie Correctional Centre, the gaol at which I work, for two years prior to his release. He was a hard worker and would occupy his days doing shifts both morning and afternoon in the metal welding workshop where he received much praise from the overseers. I had regular contact with him over this two-year period, during which he stated that he was very focused on living a clean life, staying away from criminal people from his past, and not returning to gaol.

- *I have always been housed in maximum security gaols because I am classified as an escapee. This escapee classification has meant that I cannot be housed in minimum security gaols where security is a lot less than in maximum security gaols. This has meant that better job opportunities have not been available to me before coming to Macquarie. Not in a million years could I have imagined that I could be living the life I am living now. I am working, I am happy and I am free. My life has had a complete change, it's like it has turned around and done a complete 360. Sometimes I get upset with myself that I had not done this sooner. I have spent so much of my life just wasting time.*

- *When you are in gaol you don't really have a life. There is no quality of life. If you think that you do then you are really only kidding yourself. There are people who try to make it part of their life. But being in gaol is no life at all and if you accept that being in there is your life then you are lowering yourself and not having any motivation to build yourself a better life. When you in are gaol it's the same things happening repeatedly. It is the same routine one day after the next. Gaol is very repetitive. It is much better to find things that challenge you. Life in Macquarie is not repetitive. You can get up and go to work where you learn new skills and there are so many different things to do there .*

- *I have spent most of my adult life in gaol. In and out all the time, it just never stopped. I am 45 years old now and I have spent 21 years in gaol. It is now six months since I have been released from gaol, and this is the longest time, in all of the past 21 years, that I have been out of gaol. Imagine that? It all just seems incredible. That I would just get out, start mixing*

THE INTERVIEW

with the same people, chasing drugs, doing crimes like break and enters to get money. You see, I am an ex-drug addict and that has been a big problem in my life. When you are using drugs it just seems that crime goes with it. The people you hang around with are committing crime and you just go along with them and do the same things.

- The first month after I was released was really hard. I was put up in temporary accommodation a few nights here and there. Then I was put into a hostel type of accommodation. It was full of drug addicts and users. I did not want to risk staying there, they were just the type of people that I wanted to avoid. By this time I had been working for a few weeks since my release from gaol and had saved up a bit of money. I had enough money to pay for myself and I chose to stay in a motel room. In a motel I was by myself and I was able to do my own thing. I could avoid those people that might lead me to slip up. This worked well until I was able to find more permanent accommodation which is where I live now. The place was fully furnished and that also helped me out a lot too because I didn't need to buy furniture.

- I chose to do this for myself. I could have gone and stayed at my brother's place but I wanted to get away from all the things that might unstick me from the focus I was trying to maintain. I feel that I am my own worst enemy. I felt if I had gone to my brother's house my life would have spiralled downhill. I decided that I wanted to stay away from people and situations that would lead me down the wrong path and I knew that if I did that, I would end up going back to gaol again.

- My parole officer has been helpful for me. Parole has allowed me to make my own decisions and they have not bound me up with rules. My parole officer has been very helpful and understanding. We came to this agreement together. I said to my parole officer, "Please just let me have a go at this. Give me enough freedom to prove to you that I can do this. If I do stuff up, then I totally understand that you will come and get me then." They did do this for me, and it has turned out well for both of us.

- I have had support from the gaol chaplain. That support has helped me enormously, without that help it would have been hard for me. I am a person that does not like to ask for help. I want to do everything for myself. But the support from the chaplain has really helped me a lot. The chaplain has helped me with finding a place to live, getting to shops and work, and has helped me socially too because I now attend a weekly men's group at the church.

- I think everyone that leaves prison needs some type of support. Even if it's just someone to talk to as a friend because if you want to leave your old friends in your past you need to find some people who can be your new friends.

- I decided that I did not want to attend meeting groups like AA or NA. I do realise that these can offer support to people trying to abstain from drugs or alcohol. But I had decided that these were not for me because they were full of the type of people (ex-drug addicts) that I wanted to totally avoid. I thought that I may become vulnerable and I didn't want to go anywhere where drug addicts hang out. I really did not want to slip up this time around so it was important for me to not come in contact with those type of people.

THE INTERVIEW

- I am happy living here in regional NSW and I have no desire to go and live back in Sydney, this is my home now. I will go back to visit but not live there. I keep in contact with my family. I FaceTime with my mother nearly every day. She has said many times to me that she is very proud of me now, and of course that makes me feel proud of myself. I am proud of myself because I have achieved something with my life now and years ago, I would never been able to envisage this wonderful life that I am living now.

- During my lifetime I feel that there have been many times when I have wanted to change before but I have never really been given the opportunity. I have not had the skills. MCC (Macquarie Correctional Centre) really gave me the opportunity to change. I feel that many people (inmates) want to change but they just are not given the right opportunities. If there were more training opportunities in gaols, other people would be able to come out and get work.

- I really wanted to change and this time MCC set me up for a successful release. I had just completed an EQUIPS Addictions program three days before my release so all that information was fresh in my mind. I had a job lined up. I was released from gaol on the Friday and I started work the following Tuesday. Having a job is a really key thing for success.

- When you are released you need to have someone to talk to....that helped me a lot. I think that you need someone as a support. Not someone in authority like parole or police officer, but someone who can be more of a friend for you. You need a support person that is not parole-based, not someone in authority but more friendship-based, a peer support person is best.

Interview about Macquarie Correctional Centre (referred to as either Macquarie CC or MCC)

- In a gaol like Macquarie CC the big difference is that it doesn't feel like a maximum-security gaol. I think that it is better than a minimum-security gaol. There are so many opportunities offered to you in at Macquarie CC. MCC is different, it makes you think. It makes you think that you can have a better life. A good thing about Macquarie CC is the way you live with 25 other people. When I went there, I thought that I wouldn't like it but the longer I stayed there, I did start to like it. If you want to talk to someone about something instead of having one person to talk to, you have 25 people in your pod to talk to. I think that there should be more gaols like MCC because if you really want to change you can in a place like MCC. It teaches you living skills. It's like at MCC, they teach you how to live and look after yourself. The BBQ meat packs mean that you get to cook your own food, and that is a good skill to learn. At other maximum-security gaols you have no opportunities while at MCC you have plenty of opportunities. I've taken the opportunity and run with it. I am proud of myself.

- The officers at MCC are good. I don't know if they train them a different way or if they must pass a special test to work there, but the MCC staff treat you different there. All the staff there are good; the overseers, the Sapos, the officers, everyone. The overseers in engineering were good – they let you run your own race. The senior overseer did all the background work to line me up to get a job. He found a manufacturing unit that was doing that same sort of work that we were doing in the gaol workshop. Things like farm equipment, he saw my good work ethic. And then he went out of his way to help find me employment. I never would have believed that I would gain all these skills. I never could have imagined that I would have been able to gain the skills that I did in the engineering unit. I could not have believed that I would be able to operate a laser cutter and use a laser bed.

- My new boss on the outside has been really good to me, and he is happy with the work that I am doing. He has been very supportive and is going to write a letter of support for me at getting my driver's licence. We do some work off-site, and he says that it would be an advantage if I had my licence. I have never held a driver's licence in my life, it would mean so much to me. I got my learner's permit when I was 16 years old. I really want to get my licence; I have saved up money to buy a car. These are things that I only used to dream about.

- I received a Cert II in Engineering while in custody. That has meant that I have enough skills to work in the welding workshop and I can do everything that my boss requires me to do. He is also very supportive and has said that he will pay for me to continue and gain a trade qualification in welding. I would like to complete this qualification in the future.

- I feel that there are a lot of inmates in custody that are looking for opportunities to turn their life around. I think that it would be about 40% of them are looking for these opportunities. I feel that having officers that are able to see the potential in inmates is important. They need to encourage and guide these inmates towards a better future. The government spends a lot of money on police and resources to lock criminals away. I feel that the same sort of money could be spent helping inmates that have been released from custody, on things like inmate rehabilitation. Supporting these people when they are released from gaol would be a better way to spend the public's money. I feel that if this is done right then it might stop those same people ever returning to custody and then the cycle is stopped totally.

- It does not matter how old you are, "it's never too late to change".

- Gaining skills while I was in gaol was invaluable. The TAFE teacher that came into the gaol showed me important welding techniques. This has really helped me. Those things that he showed me were a critical part to me gaining my Cert II in Engineering. I only have to complete one more year and then I will be fully qualified with a Cert III in S & P (structural and pressure).

- I like working – it keeps me occupied. I don't want to have too much spare time on my hands.

- I feel that making the person aware of their abilities is a good way to help them to think about changing their criminal lifestyle. Giving them a chance. Trusting in them and believing that they have the ability to change and lead a better life. Believing in them and highlighting to them that it is possible for them to lead a better life. That they are so much better than the life they have been leading. When they felt that people (inmates) have a sense that other people are believing in them, then it helps them to believe in themself. They don't want to let the people down who have supported them and by doing that they are also not letting themselves down.

- *I believe that you must want to change. You have to take those opportunities that are offered to you and run with them. Like I did. I have not been given the opportunities before because I have always been in maximum security gaols. MCC changed that. It gave me so many opportunities. I took them and ran with them. Anybody can do that if they really want to.*

- *I feel that if you got first-timers (first time in gaol) able to be at MCC they would succeed and not return to gaol. Especially if they had a supportive network when they were released with employment and housing set up.*

- *There are times that I regret that I hadn't made this change earlier in my life. But I also believe if I hadn't gone through what I did in my life then I would not have become the person that I am now. I am proud of myself and the person that I am now.*

CHAPTER EIGHT

THE END IS JUST THE BEGINNING

―――――――― ♦◇♦ ――――――――

The end of an inmate's time spent in gaol is often filled with many mixed emotions. They are obviously excited at the thought of being released and being able to see their family and friends, but they often become anxious as their release date gets closer and closer. The people who they have been talking to on the phone for years are now standing next to them. How will these people respond to them? The gang of mates that were a big part of their life before entering gaol haven't had much contact with them while they were in gaol, and the inmate may be questioning, "Are these people really my friends?" These same people will be on his doorstep, or in contact with him, very soon after his release. They will want to celebrate with him and pick up their lives together where they left off before he was arrested. This inmate has been trying to put new steps in place to start a new life away from crime while he has been in gaol, but the magnetic pull from these mates is very strong.

Many inmates who spend a lot of time in gaol become institutionalised. Some will even say that life on the inside is easier than life on the outside. When you are in gaol the daily chores of life are removed. A person in gaol does not have to report to Centrelink regularly. They do not have to be in the constant battle to find a place to live. They don't have to pay bills or deal with pressure from debt collectors. They are fed three times a day without going to the shops and buying their groceries. They don't have to stand in queues at the bank or at the RTA to renew their car's registration, or sit on the phone for hours talking to Medicare. All these everyday stresses are removed from their life. Their life in gaol is predictable and routine. Life on the outside has many challenges that are taken away when their freedom is taken away. So, some inmates begin to fear their release and hold a deep secret that they have become institutionalised to the very place that holds them captive. They can begin to panic at the thought of release with questions like, "Where am I going to live?", "I don't have a job lined up" or "Parole have only approved the address of my parents and I am too old to live with my parents".

I believe that these inmates need as much support and structure as possible to make the transition from gaol to community a success. A supportive parole officer can give them guidance and relieve some of their fears. Other support agencies can help them secure housing and establish a routine. If a released inmate can set themselves a routine to follow, they are able to have the feeling of structure around them in the same way that they life was structured in gaol. Having too much time on your hands is not good for anyone and boredom can lead any person to fill their time with activities that are not conducive to a positive lifestyle.

Programs have run in other states for women releasees that I think would benefit many men recently released from gaol, and having a "mentor" is a major part of these. These trial programs have shown that if these releasees establish a relationship with a mentor there are positive benefits. The mentor can help them navigate many of the challenges that I have previously mentioned. The mentor acts as a bit of a crutch and can be called upon when the releasee is struggling. They can be someone to offer advice, to be a bit of a sounding board for ideas that the releasee has come up with. They can be someone to accompany the releasee to a job interview or to sign up for a course at TAFE. The mentor could help them with shopping and getting to an appointment, or they could be someone to just catch up with, have a coffee and a chat.

As human beings we all love the security of connection. We are social beings and were not meant to live alone. We live in a community and form connections through that community. I also believe that many people have a desire to want to help their fellow beings. It gives them a sense of purpose. By contributing a little, it can make us feel that we can give something much bigger to another person. I have often read on charitable websites like World Vision that people who donate to that charity say that they receive much more than they give. It makes our heart sing and gives us a glow inside. So, if an opportunity arises for any person to become a mentor to a releasee and help guide them to a life beyond bars, think about this opportunity that could help another human being into a new beginning.

✦ ✦ ✦

REFERENCES

Merriam-Webster.com

Doranjustice.com

The TIME magazine – Content.time.com

https://allthatsinteresting.com/bastoy-prison

https://www.thestoryinstitute.com/halden

https://www.theguardian.com/

https://www.indigenousjustice.gov.au/resources/why-are-indigenous-imprisonment-rates-rising/

Australian Government - Australian Institute of Health and Welfare - https://www.aihw.gov.au/reports/australias-welfare/adult-prisoners

Therapeutic Community Programs | Alcohol Rehab

The Art of Growing Up, John Marsden

Offender Rehabilitation and Therapeutic Communities Enabling Change the TC Way, Alisa Stevens, 2012

NOTE FROM THE AUTHOR

The content in this book is the intellectual property of the author, Sue Willoughby. You may not reuse, republish, or reprint such content without my written consent. All information written is merely for informational purposes. It is not the views of Corrective Services NSW or any other authority. It is my perspective only. Much of the information contained in this book is about people that I have come into contact with but no names or identifying features are used throughout the book. I have deliberately obscured identifying features for both legal and moral reasons.

While the information in this book has been verified to the best of my abilities, I cannot guarantee that there are no mistakes or errors. Although I have made every effort to ensure that the information in this book was correct at press time, I do not assume and hereby disclaims any liability to any party for any loss, damage, or disruption caused by errors or omissions, whether such errors or omissions result from negligence, accident, or any other cause.

This book reflects the opinions and experiences of myself only.

www.ingramcontent.com/pod-product-compliance
Lightning Source LLC
Chambersburg PA
CBHW030043100526
44590CB00011B/317